DISCARD

HARVARD HONORS THESES IN ENGLISH

Number 11

SAILING TO BYZANTIUM

SAILING TO BYZANTIUM

*A Study in the Development of the Later
Style and Symbolism in the Poetry
of William Butler Yeats*

BY

J. P. O'DONNELL

OCTAGON BOOKS

A DIVISION OF FARRAR, STRAUS AND GIROUX

New York   1977

Copyright, 1939 by the President and Fellows of Harvard College

Reprinted 1971
by special arrangement with Harvard University Press

Second Octagon printing 1977

OCTAGON BOOKS
A DIVISION OF FARRAR, STRAUS & GIROUX, INC.
19 Union Square West
New York, N.Y. 10003

LIBRARY OF CONGRESS CATALOG CARD NUMBER: 70-120652
ISBN 0-374-96141-7

Manufactured by Braun-Brumfield, Inc.
Ann Arbor, Michigan
Printed in the United States of America

ACKNOWLEDGMENT

The Macmillan Company of New York City has generously granted permission to make use of the various quotations from the works of William Butler Yeats, which are fully protected by copyright.

Mr. O'Donnell and the Harvard University Press wish to acknowledge the courtesy of the original publishers in making this material available for the purposes of the present essay.

PREFACE

When the late Senator Yeats received the Nobel Award in Literature, the President of the Swedish Academy presented him with a medal. After the ceremony the poet, whose mind sees all as symbol, fondles it in his hand:

All is over, and I am able to examine my medal, its charming, decorative, academic design. French in manner, a work of the 'nineties. It shows a young man listening to a Muse, who stands young and beautiful with a great lyre in her hand, and I think as I examine it, 'I was good-looking once like that young man, but my unpractised verse was full of infirmity, my Muse old as it were; and now I am old and rheumatic, and nothing to look at, but my Muse is young. I am even persuaded that she is like those Angels in Swedenborg's vision, and moves perpetually toward the day-spring of her youth.'

William Butler Yeats published his *Collected Works* in 1908. That he has written all of his best poetry since that date, critics are in almost unanimous agreement. It is the purpose of this essay to trace that amazing development. Even such a professed lover

PREFACE

of his early verse as George Russell once compared the poet's work to that marriage-feast in the Scriptures, where the best wine was kept until the last. Yeats, with a more unchristened heart than his friend AE, turns the metaphor to his own purpose to tell us much the same thing: —

> . . . now
> I bring full-flavoured wine out of a barrel found
> Where seven Ephesian topers slept and never knew
> When Alexander's empire past, they slept so sound.

J. P. O.

Cambridge, Mass.,
June, 1939.

I

THE CELTIC TWILIGHT

I made it out of a mouthful of air

At the conclusion of *A Portrait of the Artist as a Young Man* Stephen Dedalus makes an entry in his diary:

Michael Robartes remembers forgotten beauty and, when his arms wrap her round, he presses in his arms the loveliness which has long faded from the world. Not this. Not at all. I desire to press in my arms the loveliness that has not yet come into the world.[1]

And so James Joyce, alias Stephen Dedalus, goes forth to forge in the smithy of his soul the "uncreated conscience of his race." A striking change came over Ireland at the turn of the last century, and this change is reflected in the literature of the period. Michael Robartes and his friends, with their interest in leprichauns, Gaelic legend, and old wives' tales, had endeavored to make Ireland romantic to herself. The succeeding generation "overwhelmed by responsibility, began to seek psychological truth." [2]

SAILING TO BYZANTIUM

Michael Robartes is William Butler Yeats, or rather that Willy Yeats whom Katherine Tynan once described in her memoirs, escorting her down Piccadilly with his umbrella swaying in one hand and reciting, absent-mindedly, lines from Shelley's *Sensitive Plant*.[3] In his *Autobiographies* the older Yeats has given us an equally amusing picture of himself in those days; walking through London with the artificial stride of Hamlet, and stopping at shop-windows to see why his own sailor-tie didn't flow in the breeze like Byron's tie in the picture. "I was always planning," he tells us, "some great gesture, putting the whole world into one scale of the balance and my soul into the other and imagining that the whole world somehow kicked the beam."[4] Small wonder that George Moore remarked: "In writing *Patience*, Gilbert thought he was copying Oscar Wilde, whereas actually he was drawing Willy Yeats out of the womb of time."[5]

On another occasion Willy, very homesick for Sligo, was walking down Fleet Street when he heard a little tinkle of water and saw a fountain in a shop-window, balancing upon its jet a little ball. A memory of lake water flashed across his mind, and from this experience arose what is probably the best known of Yeats's early poems — *The Lake Isle of Innisfree* — "my first lyric with anything in its rhythms of my own music":[6]

The Lake Isle of Innisfree

I will arise and go now, and go to Innisfree,
And a small cabin build there, of clay and wattles made:
Nine bean-rows will I have there, a hive for the honey-bee,
And live alone in the bee-loud glade.

And I shall have some peace there, for peace comes dropping slow,
Dropping from the veils of the morning to where the cricket sings;
There midnight's all a glimmer, and noon a purple glow,
And evening a full of linnet's wings.

I will arise and go now, for always night and day
I hear lake-water lapping with low sounds by the shore;
While I stand on the roadway, or on the pavements gray,
I hear it in the deep heart's core.

To criticize this poem (for its inversions, conventional archaisms, etc.) would be to make a hash of nightingales' tongues. All is supernal loveliness. *Innisfree* reveals the youthful poet as a master of technique; haunting rhythms and felicitous phrasing create the charming atmosphere of this poem. Almost by itself this piece marked Yeats as one of the most promising among the poets of the 'nineties — "a more delicate and more Irish Wordsworth."[7] And yet at the same time one catches in this poem distinct overtones of ennui, a certain *taedium vitae* which places it definitely in the decade of peacock-feathers and cucumber sandwiches.

When Robert Louis Stevenson first read *Innisfree*, he penned an enthusiastic note to the author from far-off Vailima, in Samoa:

> Long since when I was a boy I remember the emotions with which I repeated Swinburne's *Poems and Ballads*. Some ten years ago a similar spell was cast over me by Meredith's *Love in the Valley* . . . it may interest you to know that I have a third time fallen into slavery; this is to your poem called *The Lake Isle of Innisfree*. It is so quaint and airy, simple, artful and eloquent to the heart — but I seek words in vain. Enough that 'always night and day I hear lake-water lapping with low sounds on the shore. . . .'[8]

But to a young modern poet, Stephen Spender, the same poem summons up rather the picture of "a young man reclining on a yellow satin sofa." [9] The reader of today will agree with Spender. The poem does contain an element of enervating weariness of which Yeats in his old age seems incapable — "there would be a roar of thunder, a flash, and he would be off."

When in 1904 Paul Elmer More called Yeats "a decadent without moral degeneration" [10] he made a pertinent observation. During the period of the 'nineties most of those companions of the *Cheshire Cheese*, with whom Yeats "flung roses riotously" in London — Wilde, Dowson, Francis Thompson and Lionel Johnson — were dying off at an alarming rate. Yeats himself suffered a violent sickness and long period of recuperation. His poetry, too, becomes more and more decadent; having lost the first lyric impulse, he began refining away his art. The poems in *The Wind Among the Reeds* (1899) are on the whole inferior to his earlier verse; an endeavor "to capture some high impalpable mood in a net of obscure images." [11] He revises his play, *The Shadowy Waters*, some twenty-odd times, and this incessant revision and dissatisfaction reveal that Yeats, like

Keats with his *Hyperion*, had reached a poetic impasse. Shortly after the turn of the century one may date the death of still another of the *fin de siècle* decadents — Willy Yeats.

As a matter of fact, the requiem services were actually held — a typically Irish mock-keening scene — and are recorded gleefully by George Moore in his *Hail and Farewell*.[12] According to Moore, Yeats walked into the National Library one afternoon and met John Eglinton. Eglinton is now repeating to a group of Dublin writers the conversation: "He told me he was collecting his writing for a complete edition, a library edition in ten or twelve volumes. . . . He said to me 'Ah that style! I made it myself.'"

AE has said that a literary movement consists of five or six people who live in the same town and hate each other cordially. And, as Moore remarks, if the group was not really sorry that Yeats's inspiration was declining, they were genuinely interested to discover the cause of it. All of Yeats's utterances on the subject of style are repeated. AE suggests that his search for a conscious style ruined his art, but Gogarty, or someone else present, replies that he has no style, neither bad nor good, for he has ceased writing. Finally Moore himself turns to Arthur Symons and pronounces sentence: "His inspiration is at an end, for he talks about how he is going to write."

George Moore was wrong. The fact that Yeats was worried over the problem of style was actually to make him a better poet. In 1903, for example, we find Yeats writing, "I am trying to put a less dream-burthened will into my work." [13] Moore's criticism of Yeats's early work is, on the other hand, quite acute. He noticed the contrast between the "dream-burthened will" of the poetry and the actual Yeats, the man of intellect who vanquished Moore himself at many a Dublin dinner-table. This contrast leads Moore to what is a just and incisive criticism of the bulk of Yeats's early poetry:

> Yeats is thinner in his writings than in his talk; very little of himself gets into his literature — very little of it can get in, owing to the restrictions of his style; and these seemed to have crept closer in *Rosa Alchemica* (1897) inspiring me to prophesy one day to Symons that Yeats would lose himself in Mallarmé, whom he had never read.[14]

II

THE CHANGE IN STYLE

> The rhetorician would deceive his neighbors,
> The sentimentalist himself; while art
> Is but a vision of reality.
> — *Ego Dominus Tuus*

THE secret of all style is successful communication. It is "a sign of work well done, a certain energy of precision and movement." [15] Hence the value of style varies directly with the poet's ability to unite within it all the strands of his personality. A perfected style will allow the artist to play with all masks, sound all notes; emotion and intellect running together in perfect accord.

In this sense the achievement of a style is the perfection of a poet's art, and Yeats's constant preoccupation with this problem, although a subject for ridicule in Dublin, was essential to his growth as an artist. The amazing thing is that he triumphed over almost insuperable obstacles — that he evolved from a Celtic Pre-Raphaelite, wallowing in

THE CHANGE IN STYLE

the backwash of the Romantic Movement, to a modern poet of commanding stature.

For the explanation of Yeats's early development is historical. The whole *fin de siècle* movement was a reaction against Darwinian naturalism, against the conclusions implicit in scientific materialism. Yeats himself tells us that he hated Victorian science — Huxley and Tyndall — with "a monkish hate," [16] and its counterpart in art, Bastien-Lepage's "clownish peasant staring with vacant eyes at her great boots," fared no better. He was fond of quoting Paul Verlaine on Tennyson's *In Memoriam*, that "when Tennyson should have been broken-hearted, he had many reminiscences." The art-for-art's-sake devotees set out to purify poetry of all that was not poetry, and incidentally of much that was. These apostles of Pater decided, over their hashish and black coffee at the *Cheshire Cheese*, that they were against "the political eloquence of Swinburne, the psychological curiosity of Browning, and the poetical diction of everybody." [17]

Looking backwards to the decade of *The Yellow Book*, we today are prone to be a trifle condescending, dismissing it with one word — Decadence. But more than half of the artistic principles of Pater, Oscar Wilde and Willy Yeats are based on acute perception and common sense. The invasion of science into the realm of art had already proceeded too far, resulting in the journalistic, barren style of such English writers as the early Shaw and Wells. We soon hear Synge, who was no decadent, protesting against "Ibsen and Zola, describing the reality of life in joyless and pallid words." [18] Yeats realized this, but his own reaction was unfortunately in the opposite extreme. Hence a valid criticism of the bulk of his early work points to his false assumptions about the nature of poetry. Yeats's early poetry suffers from a complete lack of intellectual content, and invariably borders on sentimental escapism, as in *The Stolen Child*:

> Come away, O human child!
> To the waters and the wild
> With a faery, hand in hand,
> For the world's more full of weeping
>   than you can understand.

The Lake Isle of Innisfree, *The Song of Fergus*, and *When You are Old* reveal the

THE CHANGE IN STYLE

other general defects of the poems of the early period — over-charged color, traditional metaphors, obvious, all-pervading rhythm, unconscious drama — all defects inherited from the Romantic Movement. A poem is to be a supernal loveliness, lulling the mind into a waking trance. The later Yeats is to describe his own development as one in artistic sincerity. At this time he was but one of the last Romantics, who chose for theme "traditional loveliness," or longed

> For old, unhappy, far-off things,
> And battles long ago.

At this point, rather than define precisely the change in style that is to take place, it is perhaps better to see it in action. One poem from *In the Seven Woods* (1904) sounds a discordant note in the prevailing Yeatsian atmosphere of the volume. We find the poet hinting that

> A line will take us hours maybe . . .

the first sign that the creation without toil of the earlier poems is disappearing. The poem proceeds with an attack on

> . . . the noisy set
> Of bankers, schoolmasters, and clergymen
> The martyrs call the world.

Here for the first time we find actual speech rhythms, the language really used by men. But then the poet falls back into the old, accustomed grooves, articulating sweet sounds together. The rhythm becomes smooth-flowing, the imagery blurred, a twilight mood descends upon the reader:

> We sat grown quiet at the name of love;
> We saw the last embers of daylight die,
> And in the trembling blue-green of the sky
> A moon, worn as if it had been a shell
> Washed by time's waters as they rose and fell
> About the stars and broke in days and years.
>
> I had a thought for no one's but your ears:
> That you were beautiful and that I strove
> To love you in the old high way of love;
> That it had all seemed happy, and yet we'd grown
> As weary-hearted as that hollow moon.

This poem (*Adam's Curse*) has a two-fold significance: the introduction of the accents of living speech, stripped of poetic diction, in the short lines quoted; and the half-concealed punch in the last line of the poem. When the Romantic Poet discovers that the moon is hollow, he has reached an impasse — he can no longer write in the old high way of love.

THE CHANGE IN STYLE

If the readers of *Adam's Curse* felt uneasy at this new, harsher note in Yeats, it was probably dismissed as a moment's vagary, a wandering from the beaten path. Few could have suspected its significance as a pivotal point in Yeats's poetry. For with the publication of *The Green Helmet* in 1910, a remarkable thing has occurred. There is no doubt now as to which way the wind blows. Lines like the following must have had the effect of an exploding bombshell among whole bevies of Yeats-devotees:

> Why should I blame her that she filled my days
> With misery, or that she would of late
> Have taught to ignorant men most violent ways
> Or hurled the little streets upon the great,
> Had they but courage equal to desire? . . . [19]

One turns the page and finds the style even more arrogant and assertive, the rhythm bold, provocative and harsh:

> . . . My curse on plays
> That have to be set up in fifty ways
> On the day's war with every knave and dolt,
> Theatre business, management of men.
> I swear before the dawn comes round again
> I'll find the stable and pull out the bolt. [20]

Even the titles of the poems are indicative of the new realistic mood: *The Fascination of*

SAILING TO BYZANTIUM

What's Difficult, A Drinking Song, and *On Hearing that the Students of our New University Have Joined the Agitation Against Immoral Literature.*

There are three major factors which go far toward explaining the apparently complete about-face in Yeats's poetic technique.[21] We have already noticed George Moore remarking that very little of the real Yeats succeeded in getting into his early writing, and it is to biography that we must look for an explanation of the change that has come over the poetry. Fortunately, Yeats himself helps us here, both in the published prose of this second period (1904–1910), and also in extracts from a diary kept in 1909, and recently published. I draw on the prose as well as the poetry of this period, for Yeats's prose is certainly the most valuable commentary by a poet on his own art since Coleridge's *Biographia Literaria* and the letters of John Keats.

The first factor in the change, although the most obvious, is also perhaps the most important — the poet was growing older. T. S. Eliot has remarked that a poet runs into most difficulties after the age of twenty-

THE CHANGE IN STYLE

five.[22] Yeats was now in his thirties, and in 1908 published his *Collected Works*. It is significant that Romantic poets like Keats and Shelley died young, or, as in Wordsworth's case, should have. The young man can exploit his native genius without worrying over-much about ideas. But the unbinding of youth's dreamy load raises pertinent questions. Even Keats, shortly before his death, was becoming perplexed with his *Hyperion*, much in the same manner as was Yeats with his play *The Shadowy Waters*. We know that Keats, who in early youth longed for "a life of sensations rather than of thoughts," later came to admit that "an extensive knowledge is needful to thinking people," and that "poetry is not so fine a thing as philosophy."[23] One can only speculate as to the probable effect of Keats's rapidly maturing intellect upon his art. But with the parallel case of Yeats, as also with Goethe, we can see the process proceed to completion. It is a study in the exfoliation of style, a transition from the profuseness of Romantic dream-poetry to a highly premeditated art — almost classical in its bareness of imagery, sharp outline, and clear-cut thought-pattern. Yeats's whole life has been spent in eliminating the poetic from his verse, or rather his early "artificially induced poeticality." [24]

My mention of Goethe brings us to the second factor which has a direct bearing on the genesis of the new style. Yeats, like Goethe before him, was drawn away from his self-chosen vocation of lonely subjective artist by the pressure of public affairs — in Yeats's case the practical difficulties connected with launching the Abbey Theatre and keeping the players on the boards (*cf. ante* p. 21). The descent from the Ivory Tower — or Alchemical Temple — into the hurly-burly of modern Dublin made Yeats a public figure, and to be a public figure in the Dublin of that time "it was as necessary to carry the heart upon the sleeve as the tongue in the cheek." [25]

Yeats had always nursed the ambition to play with hostile minds as Hamlet had played, and now to avoid the brickbats — literary and political — of those turbulent days, he assumed a definite rôle, exploiting his natural histrionic tendencies. At first a defensive *alter ego*, this public posturing,

THE CHANGE IN STYLE

this deliberate cultivation of platform dramatics and "the proper gesture" soon became an integral part of the Yeats-legend. Although this pose made many personal enemies for him in everyday life, to Yeats as a poet such public experiences were invaluable. It gave him what was conspicuous by its absence in the early poetry — poise — the self-assurance of a mature intellect sharpened by combat in the public forum.

> Es bildet ein Talent sich in der Stille
> Ein Charakter im Strome der Welt.

As a poet Yeats had been a man of solitude, part Axel, part Shelleyan Alastor, aloof and subjective; but as an Irishman he was by definition gregarious. When Yeats, after his fifteen years in the literary wars, retired for some time from the political arena, he was now able to play with all Masks. His later poetry maintains at all times a conscious theatrical discipline.

Those who know the history of the Abbey Theatre in its formative years will realize that I speak of Yeats as the spokesman of a cultural movement, warring against middle-class cant, rather than of Yeats the dramatist. His own plays of this period share the defects of his early poetry — obvious, all-pervading rhythm:

> Bend down your faces, Oona and Aleel
> I gaze upon them as the swallow gazes
> Upon the nest under the eave, before
> She wander the loud waters.[26]

As Yeats continued to write plays his dramatic style did, however, tend in the direction of living, passionate speech, as it does at times in *Deirdre*; hence his experience in the theatre itself made some contribution to the change which came about in style.

But far more important is the change which came over Yeats's thought in the period 1895–1910. The poet of *Innisfree* set out to make Ireland romantic to herself. In 1895 he writes:

> It is pleasant to dream that Irish poetry will some day be great enough to lead a world sick with theories to those sweet well-waters of primeval poetry, upon whose edge still linger the brotherhoods of wisdom, the immortal moods.[27]

This was a pleasant dream, couched in the extravagant style Yeats learned of Pater. One answer to this dream is James Joyce's *Ulysses*. But Yeats, inspired by Victor

THE CHANGE IN STYLE

Hugo's dictum that "in the theatre the mob becomes a people," cherished the grandiose vision of a Unity of Culture. He felt that the budding Nationalist Movement could be made the handmaiden of Literature, and with this in mind he wrote *The Countess Cathleen* — a play in the best shamrock tradition. But at the opening performance the audience hissed:

A libel on Ireland. . . . Blasphemy. . . . We never sold our Faith. . . . No Irish woman ever did it. . . . We want no amateur atheists. . . . We want no budding Buddhists. . . . [28]

The Cardinal of Dublin denounced the "heresy" that

> . . . The Light of Lights
> Looks always on the motive, not the deed.

which, ironically enough, is good Catholic doctrine. Already Yeats must have sensed what was to come — art made tongue-tied by authority. With the help of the Nationalists Yeats fought the rancour aroused by his own harmless play, and succeeded in securing a hearing for the Irish Dramatic Movement. Then came Synge with his *Playboy of the Western World*. This time

Sinn Fein and Roman Catholic Dublin joined forces. As Yeats stood in the back of the Abbey during the riots, his dream-structure of "Ireland and the Arts" crumbled on all sides. Synge took the disgraceful affair more philosophically than Yeats, who struck back:

On Those Who Hated
"The Playboy of the Western World," 1907

> Once, when midnight smote the air
> Eunuchs ran through Hell and met
> On every crowded street to stare
> Upon great Juan riding by:
> Even like these to rail and sweat
> Staring upon his sinewy thigh.

The night of the Playboy Riot [29] is a definite turning-point in Yeats's poetic career. It lingers in his memory for several years; we find a prose version of the above epigram in the diary kept in 1909. For Synge symbolizes in Yeats's mind what was now to be his own ideal:

> He preserved *the integrity of art in an age of reasons and purposes* . . . he was the more hated because he gave his country what it needed, an unmoved mind where there is a perpetual last day, a trumpeting, and coming up to judgment.[30]

THE CHANGE IN STYLE

From this time on Yeats's conception of the rôle of the artist in modern society becomes fixed. He deliberately cultivates a lonely, haughty, aristocratic art, and one sees his style mature remarkably during the period 1907–1914. He becomes an ascetic — "not of women or of wine, but of the newspapers." [31] Looking back on this seminal phase of his development, the older Yeats writes in his *Autobiographies*:

I had already flitting through my head . . . a conviction that we should satirize rather than praise, that original virtue arises from the discovery of evil. If we were, as I had dreaded, declamatory, loose and bragging, we were but the better fitted, — that declared and measured — to create unyielding personality, manner at once cold and passionate, daring long pre-meditated act; and if bitter beyond all the people of the world, we might yet lie — that too declared and measured — nearest the honeyed comb.[32]

This passage is at once a penetrating statement of Yeats's creed as an artist in Ireland, and an admirable example of that cold, clear, Galway rock style which is now about to enter his work. Wilfred Owen stated a view similar to Yeats's when he announced that "all a poet can do today is warn." For what can the artist of the present do but shore up his fragments against an age in which

> The best lack all conviction, while the worst
> Are filled with passionate intensity

We come now to the third and dominant element in *The Green Helmet* poems which makes the breach with the early style complete. Yeats had from the beginning been a love-poet, brooding upon love's bitter mystery in terms of "the poet to his beloved":

> I bring you with reverent hands
> The book of my numberless dreams
> White woman that passion has worn
> As the tide wears the dove-gray sands.[33]

To measure the growth of Yeats as an artist, one has only to compare this charming bit of lavender and old lace, out of Swinburne, with the classical fierceness, the *saeva indignatio* of *No Second Troy* (1910):

What could have made her peaceful with a mind
That nobleness made simple as a fire,
With beauty like a tightened bow, a kind
That is not natural in an age like this,
Being high and solitary and most stern?
Why, what could she have done, being what she is?
Was there another Troy for her to burn?

THE CHANGE IN STYLE

Even casual readers of Yeats's poetry will observe that he returns constantly to ponder,

> Does the imagination dwell the most
> Upon a woman won or woman lost?

This is a rhetorical question — the answer is known to all of us. In his youth Yeats felt that

If I am sincere and make my language natural . . . I shall, if good or bad luck make my life interesting, be a great poet; for it will no longer be a matter of literature at all.[34]

Yeats met this bad luck sooner than he expected. Apparently his passionate attachment to his Laura was returned "with scarce a pitying look," or what is perhaps worse, she regarded him as a friend. The woman of Yeats's love-poetry was no dream woman, she was as real as Dante's Beatrice. Maud Gonne was that rare, queenly type of passionate woman, a Deirdre or an Irish Jeanne d'Arc. The most handsome woman in Ireland, some regarded her as the reigning beauty of Europe; to Yeats she was the most beautiful woman in the world, a reincarnation of Homer's paragon. The classical symbolism is peculiarly appropriate. Many years later, when writing *A Vision* (1925) Yeats, ostensibly describing Helen of Troy, has still in his mind's eye the image of Maud Gonne:

> Here are born those women most touching in their beauty. Helen was of this phase; and she comes before the mind's eye elaborating a delicate personal discipline, as though she would make her whole life an image of a unified antithetical energy. While seeming an image of softness and quiet, she draws perpetually upon glass with a diamond.[35]

Yeats proposed several times to Maud Gonne, and she refused him on eminently practical grounds — he was a poet and she was a revolutionary. In Yeats's own terms of the inevitable conflict between the artist and "an age of reasons and purposes," any marriage would have ended in mutual incompatibility. According to Yeats, Maud Gonne insisted that she must marry "some poor lout" in the Nationalist Movement (one suspects the term is Yeats's own).[36] She later married Colonel Macbride, who was executed during The Trouble. Yeats spoils what is otherwise his finest occasional poem, *Easter 1916*, by still referring to Macbride as

THE CHANGE IN STYLE

a "drunken, vainglorious lout" — the one distinct note of sour grapes in his poetry. One can admire Yeats as an artist while sympathizing with Maud Gonne as a woman, particularly when she writes to her poet-suitor:

> Ah yes, you are happy without me, because you make beautiful poetry out of what you call your unhappiness and you are happy in that. Marriage would be such a dull affair. Poets should never marry. The world should thank me for not marrying you.[37]

Lips only sing when they cannot kiss. Yeats and Maud Gonne went their separate ways. Years later, when the performance of Sean O'Casey's *The Plow and the Stars* was broken up by another Abbey riot (1927), William Butler Yeats stood on the stage shouting "Long live Ireland and freedom of expression" for a play he didn't particularly like, while outside marched resolute Irish Republican pickets, led by a sixty-five-year-old shrill-voiced firebrand — Maud Gonne. Here in dramatic fashion was being enacted virtually the last act of the drama of modern Ireland, with Yeats and his erstwhile phoenix as protagonists.

SAILING TO BYZANTIUM

I have been analyzing the poems of *The Green Helmet* and *Responsibilities* (1907–1914) in terms of the appearance of a new style. The poems into which the Maud Gonne motif of "returned but unrequited love" enters (*A Woman Homer Sung, Reconciliation*, and *When Helen Lived*) are in general superior artistically to the other short poems. But as end piece to the work of this transition period, Yeats appends a poem which is at once a description and an actual example of the new style toward which he is working:

A Coat

> I made my song a coat
> Covered with embroideries
> Out of old mythologies
> From heel to throat;
> But the fools caught it,
> Wore it in the world's eyes
> As though they'd wrought it.
> Song, let them take it,
> For there's more enterprise
> In walking naked.

III

THE DANTESQUE PERIOD

> I have no speech but symbol, the pagan speech I made amid the dreams of youth.

In emphasizing the breach between the earlier and the later work of Yeats, one is apt to convey the impression that the poet's first thirty years were all spent wandering aimlessly down Hodos Chameliontos; and that suddenly, some time around 1907, he became a new poet. But then we are encountered by the fact that Yeats has been from the beginning a symbolist poet (as Mr. Wilson demonstrates in *Axel's Castle*), and that in this respect there is an underlying continuity in Yeats's poetry. Since I intend to discuss the later poetry in terms of its symbolism, it is important to attempt a definition of that rather ambiguous critical term. Although the poetry of Yeats's maturity stems partly from the symbolist theories he and others expounded in the 'nineties, his later symbolism is in reality almost an altogether different thing. One still speaks of the symbolism of Yeats's later poetry, but it is a far cry from *fin de siècle Symbolisme*.

One finds Yeats as early as 1897 remarking that "the Symbolical movement . . . is the only movement that is saying new things."[38] He was then fresh from those discussions in Paris with men like Verlaine, although he apparently never met Mallarmé, the high priest of the Symbolist Movement.[39] Poetry is to be a distillation, the essence of impersonal beauty; the poet "captures some high impalpable mood in a net of obscure images."[40] All is suggestion — "le suggérer, voilà le rêve. C'est le parfait usage de ce mystère qui constitue le symbole."[41] The Symbolists were not concerned with ideas but were partakers at the banquet of moods. The precise shading in color, the correct musical rhythm, and a limited poetic vocabulary were all part of the Symbolist technique; but the private symbol — the more private the better — was the *pièce de résistance*. Mallarmé's influence accounts for an occasional horrible green parrot or dark leopard in Yeats's poetry.

THE DANTESQUE PERIOD

The esoteric nature of the poetry of the French Symbolistes soon led Yeats to abandon their obscurantist technique for more fruitful fields. He still believed in the magic of the symbol, but was seeking at the same time a more coherent body of traditional symbols when he fortunately looked homeward toward Ireland. Now we find in his poetry a Druid symbolism that is less arbitrary: Avalon, the silver apples of the moon, Fergus with his brazen car, the valley of the Black Pig, the wood-woman whose lover was changed to a blue-eyed hawk — all have a meaning derived from Irish mythology. The hound with one red ear, for example, symbolizes eternal pursuit of an impossible goal.[42] Here was a world in which Irishmen at least knew their way around, and we must not forget that at this point (1895–1904) Yeats was in search of an Irish audience, an audience which never read Mallarmé or Rimbaud.

Here, however, I disagree with those critics who, like Edmund Wilson,[43] maintain that Yeats's symbolism was imported from France, sprinkled with Pater, and planted in Ireland. Yeats was writing in the English language, and would hardly have neglected the most important symbolist of them all — William Blake. We know that Yeats spent four years editing the *Prophetic Books* (1889–1893) and thus steeped his mind in Blake's world of the imagination. His poetry of the 'nineties is as close to Blake as it is to any contemporary literary movement. Such symbols as the Secret Rose, the Little Red Fox and the Sailing Seven have been borrowed directly. And the naïve rhythms, the short four-line stanza-form of the *Songs of Innocence and Experience* make their reappearance in *The Rose* and *The Wind Among the Reeds*. Another parallel trait is, as one critic points out, a disregard for material distinctions between classes of things in the world — "virgins and lambs and worms and stones and stars are all equally likely to be sighing or singing or weaving a shadowy cloak." [44] In one of Yeats's latest poems one still finds echoes of Blake in the refrain

Sang a bone upon the shore.

Yeats is always closer to Blake than to Mallarmé. When he speaks of Symbolism in his *Essays* he is thinking usually of Blake's

Tiger or Sunflower, or "O Rose thou art sick." [45] The symbol as we find it in Blake differs from the "metaphors detached from their subjects" [46] of the *fin de siècle* Symbolistes. It has meaning. And it differs from the traditional metaphor, or simile, in that the analogy between symbol and thing symbolized holds at more than one point. As a perfect example of what Yeats meant at this time by an emotional symbol we find him quoting and commenting on his favorite lines in Burns:

The white moon is setting behind the white wave,
And Time is setting with me, O!

Take away from these lines the whiteness of the moon and of the waves, whose relation to the setting of Time is too subtle for the intellect, and you take away from them their beauty. But, when all are together, moon and wave and whiteness and setting Time and the last melancholy cry, they evoke an emotion which cannot be evoked by any other arrangement of color and sounds and forms.[47]

In the poems from 1910 onward we find Yeats speaking more and more in a new symbolic language. Gone are the green eyes of the dark leopards of the moon. The Celtic mythology has also either been laid aside or exhausted, for in the 'nineties even the Irish symbolism had been intentionally vague, free from "contaminating ideas." Yeats had certainly found the poetry of ideas in his master, Blake, but was sidetracked by the *ignis fatuus* of his youth — the pure poetry of the art-for-art's-sake movement. Now, in *The Magi* and *The Dolls*, we find the Blakean fusion of emotion with intellect, with this difference: because Blake was a true mystic, his poetry has a certain aura of timelessness, whereas Yeats always writes with one eye on his own times. He plunders the past for symbols, but he uses them as a touchstone to apply to the present.

Those enraged dolls, for example, are more than dolls in a doll-maker's house. At first sight what we have is a dramatic lyric with a symbolic but hidden meaning. One then reads *The Magi* and comprehends the significance of its companion poem and the skillful use of counterpoint. The dolls become assembly-line automatons, living in the doll-house of modern civilization, which is, in Blake's terms, "something other than human life." (Quoted by Yeats, *Plays and*

THE DANTESQUE PERIOD

Controversies, p. 98.) The wife of the doll-maker has given birth to a child, a noisy and filthy thing. This creative impudence is a disgrace to the dolls and to their producer, the doll-maker. So the mother apologizes — "my dear, O dear, it was an accident." Over against this scene we have the Magi, complementary forms of those enraged dolls, the wisemen of the East:

> . . . hoping to find once more
> Being by Calvary's turbulence unsatisfied,
> The uncontrollable mystery on the bestial floor.

By combining the traditional symbol of the Magi with his own creation, the dolls, Yeats plays off in a Flaubertian contrast, the grandeur of the past against our own age of hollow men.

The Magi

Now as at all times I can see in the mind's eye,
In their stiff, painted clothes, the pale unsatisfied ones
Appear and disappear in the blue depth of the sky
With all their ancient faces like rain-beaten stones,
And all their helms of silver hovering side by side,
And all their eyes still fixed, hoping to find once more,
Being by Calvary's turbulence unsatisfied,
The uncontrollable mystery on the bestial floor.

SAILING TO BYZANTIUM

The Dolls

A doll in the doll-maker's house
Looks at the cradle and bawls:
'That is an insult to us.'
But the oldest of all the dolls,
Who had seen, being kept for show,
Generations of his sort,
Outscreams the whole shelf: 'Although
There's not a man can report
Evil of this place,
The man and the woman bring
Hither, to our disgrace,
A noisy and filthy thing.'
Hearing him groan and stretch
The doll-maker's wife is aware
Her husband has heard the wretch,
And crouched by the arm of his chair,
She murmers into his ear,
Head upon shoulder leant:
'My dear, my dear, O dear,
It was an accident'

Here we have the symbolist technique functioning at its very best: its irony, its imaginative power, and above all the subtle play of overtone and suggestion. Have the mother and child of the doll-maker's house any relation to that other mother with her child in the manger — the bestial floor? And surely traditional Christianity has "dwindled to a box of toys," [48] for

THE DANTESQUE PERIOD

are not even the Magi unsatisfied by Calvary's turbulence? At the same time one notes they are described as "hopeful." The strength of the dramatic lyric, as Day Lewis observes, lies in its manifold implications.[49]

The symbolism of this middle period of Yeats's work differs from the earlier unicorns and Druid moons in that it becomes a direct approach to experience rather than an escape into Tir-nan-oge, never-never land. When Mr. I. A. Richards accuses Yeats of retiring behind black velvet curtains and "making a violent repudiation not merely of current civilization but of life itself," [50] I confess I am puzzled. And when he goes on to add that "Yeats's sensibility is a development off the main track and it is this which seems to make it minor poetry in a sense in which Mr. Hardy's best work and T. S. Eliot's *The Wasteland* are major poetry," one wonders whether it is Mr. Yeats or Mr. Richards who is the "pathetic spectacle." The best answer I can make to Mr. Richards is to discuss the poetry on his own terms — repudiation of current civilization and of life itself. Are the two necessarily synonymous? And how, save by suicide, does one repudiate life itself?

The poem *The Fisherman* is at once a statement and an embodiment of that "stern color and that delicate line" which is now Yeats's secret discipline. The poem has three distinct movements. The poet first sees the fisherman in the mind's eye, a study in gray — gray place on a hill, gray Connemara cloth, gray dawn. Note the deliberate climbing effect of the rhythm, the accent falling on bare, monosyllabic words. Then comes a sharp shift in emphasis, the introduction of the *leitmotif*:

> To write for my own race
> And the reality.

The thought and meter quicken, the tone now becomes haughty, scornful, arrogant, for the scene has shifted to Dublin — that blind, bitter town. Yeats in a dozen lines recounts the hectic turmoil, the drawn battles and the hatreds of the years of his youth — the Parnell controversy, the riots over Synge's *Playboy*, the rejection of Sir Hugh Lane's pictures by the Municipal Gallery, etc.:

THE DANTESQUE PERIOD

> The beating down of the wise
> And great art beaten down.

Then, in a remarkable transition, Yeats drops the jerky, bombastic accents for still another rhythm — at first a reversion to the slow, meditative lines of the opening stanza, then a gradual quickening of the thought, a holding up of the rhythmic beat, a short pause before the climax, and the poem rides out quickly to its resolution in the last line:

> . . . Before I am old
> I shall have written him one
> Poem maybe as cold
> And passionate as the dawn.

The Fisherman

> Although I can see him still,
> The freckled man who goes
> To a grey place on a hill
> In grey Connemara clothes
> At dawn to cast his flies
> It's long since I began
> To call up to the eyes
> This wise and simple man.
> All day I'd looked in the face
> What I had hoped 'twould be
> To write for my own race
> And the reality;
> The living men that I hate,
> The dead man that I loved,
> The craven man in his seat,

The insolent unreproved,
And no knave brought to book
Who has won a drunken cheer,
The witty man and his joke
Aimed at the commonest ear,
The clever man who cries
The catch-cries of the clown,
The beating down of the wise
And great Art beaten down.

Maybe a twelvemonth since,
Suddenly I began,
In scorn of this audience,
Imagining a man,
And his sun-freckled face,
And grey Connemara cloth,
Climbing up to a place
Where stone is dark under froth,
And the down-turn of his twist
When the flies drop in the stream;
A man who does not exist,
A man who is but a dream;
And cried, 'Before I am old
I shall have written him one
Poem maybe as cold
And passionate as the dawn.'

We realize that this is the poem as cold and passionate as the dawn, and that the Fisherman — the man who is but a dream — is that ideal audience toward which the poet now directs his thought.

This search for an audience is no idle quest. Yeats, some time after 1910, withdrew from the turmoil of public affairs, but many battles had left wounds, bitter memories:

> Out of Ireland have we come
> Great hatred, little room.[51]

Irish writers like Synge, and later Joyce, could ignore the mob; but Yeats's fanatic heart raged at the Philistine — the middle-class morality of Paddy and Paudeen. His peculiar intellectual honesty, plus at times a commendable pugnacity, urged Yeats constantly to defend the integrity of an artist in a country where politics was almost an art in itself. He was a follower of that fine old Fenian, John O'Leary, who had said "there are things a man must not do to save a nation," and to Yeats one of those things was to write second-rate literature, as Tom Moore had done, glorifying "convivial Ireland of the traditional smile and tear." Yeats broke with the sentimentalists, literary and political. From the lecture platform he would infuriate his audience by sneering at

Believe me, if all those endearing young charms
Which I gaze on so fondly today. . . .[52]

To most Irishmen this was sacrilege, and Yeats gradually became one of the best-hated figures in Dublin. He had a few chosen friends and many enemies; his personal idiosyncrasies helped to make more enemies of those who should have been his friends. By 1910, then, when it appeared that Yeats had shot his bolt in poetry, and had been defeated in the public imbroglio, there was almost general rejoicing. Yeats had apparently abandoned Cathleen ni Houlihan, and Ireland was no longer interested. He became in the public eye his own weather-worn marble Triton among the streams.

The Great War confirmed Yeats's conviction of the isolation of the artist in society. While other poets wrote stirring war poems, Yeats maintained a deliberate silence.[53] During this period, when few people read poetry and fewer still read Yeats, the latter was painstakingly analyzing his own shortcomings and forming a conception of the rôle of the artist which would resolve his own personal dilemma. Although it seemed at the time even to his friends [54] that Yeats was wandering *per amica silentia lunae*,

THE DANTESQUE PERIOD

abandoning the muse for metaphysics, poetry for prose, he emerged from his intellectual questionings a more mature and better poet. We find him groping toward a new conception of the basis of style in the *Essays* of 1915-1917, as he comes more and more to regard all art as an escape from personality.[55] The result is the formulation of the doctrine of the Mask. We had already seen Yeats moving in this direction in the poem *The Fisherman*, for the fisherman became a symbol — an objective correlative — of an austere, impersonal art. Years later Yeats is remembering this poem when he writes:

> As I look backward upon my own writing, I take pleasure alone in those verses where it seems to me I have found something hard and cold, some articulation of the image, which is the opposite of all that I am in my daily life, and all that my country is.[56]

Now, in *Ego Dominus Tuus* (1917), Yeats becomes more explicit. He had noted long before the apparent paradox in the life of an artist and in his work. John Synge, a silent, gentle, meditative man, filled his plays with voluble daredevils, with laughing, ecstatic violence; while Walter Landor, in real life a man of demoniac passion, infuses his verse with a marmorean calm. William Morris, a "happy, busy, most irascible man," describes in his poetry dim color and pensive emotion, following an indolent Muse. Yeats himself displays this duality: all gentleness and love in his early poetry, he was quite otherwise at the dinner-table or in conversation. With quite remarkable insight, Yeats now attempts an explanation of this anomaly in terms of split personality:

Hic: And yet
  The chief imagination of Christendom,
  Dante Alighieri, so utterly found himself
  That he has made that hollow face of his
  More plain to the mind's eye than any face
  But that of Christ.

Ille: And he did find himself
  Or was the hunger that had made it hollow
  A hunger for the apple on the bough
  Most out of reach? and is that spectral image
  The man that Lapo and that Guido knew?
  I think he fashioned from his opposite
  An image that might have been a stony face
  Staring upon a Bedouin's horse-hair roof
  From doored and windowed cliff, or half-
      upturned
  Among the coarse grass and the camel-dung.
  He set his chisel to the hardest stone.
  Being mocked by Guido for his lecherous life

THE DANTESQUE PERIOD

> Derided and deriving, driven out
> To climb the stair and eat that bitter bread,
> He found the unpersuadable justice, he found
> The most exalted lady loved by a man.

This concept of the Mask is itself a symbol — a symbol of self-imposed objectivity — of the subjection of the Romantic Will to a more severe discipline, preserving at the same time "the passion that is exultation and the negation of the will." [57] It enables Yeats the individualist to speak with an authority that seems actually to transcend the individual personality. He is the one modern poet who can sustain the grand manner without artificial inflation or rhetoric:

> Turning and turning in the widening gyre
> The falcon cannot hear the falconer;
> Things fall apart; the centre cannot hold;
> Mere anarchy is loosed upon the world,
> The blood-dimmed tide is loosed, and everywhere
> The ceremony of innocence is drowned;
> The best lack all conviction, while the worst
> Are full of passionate intensity.[58]

Another secret of the stern beauty of much of his poetry now is his perfection of the emotional symbol, particularly in the poems written during the trying times of Civil War:

SAILING TO BYZANTIUM

> The bees build in the crevices
> Of loosening masonry, and there
> The mother birds bring grubs and flies.
> My wall is loosening; honey-bees,
> Come build in the empty house of the stare.

As with so much of Yeats's best poetry, this piece had its origin in an actual occurrence.[59] But the poet has invested the traditional symbol of the honey-bee (industry, fertility, harmony), and the Irish stare (hatred, violence, sterility) with a universal significance; the loosening masonry becomes the crumbling walls of civilization. In another poem we hear of "brazen hawks," with "innumerable clanging wings that have put out the moon," [60] and find that Yeats has a "ring with a hawk and butterfly on it, to symbolize the straight road of logic, and so of mechanism, and the crooked road of intuition: for wisdom is a butterfly and not a gloomy bird of prey." Sometimes the symbol has an intentionally mysterious aspect — the "rude beast" that "slouches toward Bethlehem to be born," or those "indignant desert birds." One notices that, reflecting the chaos of the times, these symbols tend to embody an emotion of hatred or violence.

THE DANTESQUE PERIOD

Yeats epitomizes this mood in that wonderful line from his Civil War poem:

Vengeance on the murderers of Jacques Molay!

When Yeats turns to the intellectual or more abstract symbol, he has less success. The hawks, beasts and insolent fiends present no problem of communication. They carry an emotional charge. It adds little to one's appreciation of the poem, for example, to know that Jacques Molay "was a murdered Grand Master of the Templars, and that the cry of vengeance had been incorporated into the ritual of certain Masonic societies of the eighteenth century, and fed class hatred." [61] But when we come to such poems as *The Phases of the Moon*, and more particularly *The Double Vision of Michael Robartes*, we find an arbitrary and certainly incoherent symbolism. What, for example, is the average intelligent reader to make of that weird dance in *The Double Vision*?

This half-read wisdom of demonic images has a certain beauty, but the symbolism simply fails to come off.[62] Lesser poets can take refuge behind obscurity, but when Yeats fails to communicate, there are different reasons. When he appends to these two poems the note "To some extent I wrote these poems as a text for exposition," I feel this explains why *The Phases of the Moon* is such a bad poem. The symbolism has been dragged in, or at least put on from without. Yeats, whose "virtues are the definitions of the analytic mind," is to overcome the difficulties encountered in the poems of this period. In *The Tower* (1928) and *The Winding Stair* (1933) we find a successful, organic fusion of thought and emotion within the symbol. The remarkable thing was that Yeats, already in his late 'fifties when the poems of the early 1920's were written, reserved his triumph for old age. Had he ceased writing at this time, and been content to be a sixty-year-old, smiling, public man, we could sympathize with his impatient younger critics, Auden and MacNeice:

> Item, we leave the phases of the moon
> To Mr. Yeats to rock his bardic sleep.[63]

The phases of the moon, however, make their reappearance in Yeats's later poetry under more auspicious stars.

IV

PUBLICATION OF *A VISION*

> It is of much more importance for us to have experience than to have philosophies. Plato has said that if there be any Gods they certainly do not philosophize. — AE

ALTHOUGH Yeats was awarded the Nobel Prize in 1923, considerable time elapsed before his next volume of verse — *The Tower* — was published in 1928. Before one can discuss this later poetry, however, it is necessary to turn to Yeats's most important prose work, *A Vision*, which he wrote and published privately (1925) during intervals between his poetic labors. This book is not only the most difficult of Yeats's writings, but is also, to many critics, his most significant. A product of his maturity, it is to be regarded as a summation and integration of all the various strands of his philosophy, most of which has been scattered through his earlier prose essays. I have said this book is difficult, and much of the difficulty arises from the problem of belief. For one never knows just how seriously to take Yeats's mysticism, and in *A Vision* the supernatural element is too important to be overlooked.

All his life Yeats has wavered between mysticism and scepticism. In his youth he was fascinated by the doctrines of Madame Blavatsky, who believed that there was another globe stuck on the earth at the North Pole, and that the shape of the earth was literally a dumb-bell.[64] At another time, he tells us:

> I once visited a Cabbalist who spent the day trying to look out of the eyes of his canary, and he announced at nightfall that all things had for it color but nothing outline. His method of contemplation was probably in error.[65]

This passage is typical of many in Yeats. Trances, hypnotism, and all forms of extra-sensory perception delight his mind. He believes in them "with his imagination," however, for Yeats always leaves a margin of doubt for his intellect — "his method of contemplation was undoubtedly in error." Yeats so often has his tongue in his cheek that one suspects a large amount of mumbo-jumbo and pure blarney in his early writings on the supernatural.

PUBLICATION OF "A VISION"

In *A Vision*, however, the mysticism demands more serious attention. We are told that the content of the book was revealed to Yeats by automatic writing, "Communicators," working through his wife's mind and later during her sleep.[66] What they reveal to Yeats is a highly complicated metaphysical system — a fantastic synthesis of astrology, psychology, and the Platonic year. When Yeats offered to spend what remained of his life piecing together their scattered sentences, the Communicators answered, "no, we have come to give you metaphors for poetry."[67] It is as metaphors for poetry that the *Vision* is of interest to us. Moreover, one suspects that such was Yeats's ulterior motive in writing this strange book, for he refers to it later as but "a background for my thoughts, a painted scene."[68]

If, then, we regard *A Vision* as a stylistic arrangement of experience, we can account for the gain in self-possession and power which characterizes the poetry of *The Tower* (1928) and *The Winding Stair* (1929). In the poems of the preceding period, we have noticed, "an always personal emotion was woven into a general pattern of myth and symbol." Now that general pattern has come to a sharper focus, for Yeats has more confidence in it; and the emotion becomes less of a *cri de coeur* because of its reference to a more general external pattern. What Yeats has done is to arrive at that "unification of sensibility" which all modern poets are striving desperately to attain. Being at heart an individualist, he had to create his own system, his own mythology. Whereas T. S. Eliot worked his way back to Christianity, and some younger poets today espouse Marx via Freud, it is characteristic of Yeats that he falls back on the phases of the moon.

Much of *A Vision* is concerned with the problem of personality, particularly in its relation to the artist. Here we find in great detail a prose exposition of the doctrine of the Mask already expounded in *Ego Dominus Tuus*. Briefly, what Yeats does is to divide human personality into categories which correspond to the phases of the moon. The moon, in its orbit around the earth, passes through twenty-eight transformations. When it is nearest the sun — a symbol

PUBLICATION OF "A VISION"

of complete objectivity, the moon itself is dark; when farthest away it is full; between these two poles then, occur twenty-six phases of varying degrees of light and darkness. Yeats uses the full moon as a symbol of complete subjectivity, and classifies men according as they are predominantly subjective or objective. This metaphor is quite simple.

Yeats complicates this pattern, however, by interweaving a parallel phase — symbolism applied to history. Western civilization in the Christian era (1–2000 A.D.) passes through corresponding periods of subjective and objective, and the 2000-year cycle is broken up into two sub-cycles of a thousand years each. Add to this such terms as Daimons, Tinctures, Antithetical, Husks and Passionate Bodies, and one is tempted to describe *A Vision* as Yeats himself speaks of his Great Wheel:

. . . danced on desert sands by mysterious dancers who left the traces of their feet to puzzle the Caliph of Bagdad and his learned men.[69]

Behind all the paraphernalia of *A Vision* Yeats is really absorbed in the problem he has wrestled with throughout his life — the relationship of the individual artist to his own time. From his system it follows that a man of one individual phase will very likely be born in a different historical phase. Thus Shakespeare, a man of phase twenty, falls historically into phase sixteen. To a man of primary (objective) nature (phases twenty-two to eight) the artistic problem is relatively simple. He finds his emotional outlet by forgetting himself and plunging into the external world. Synge and Rembrandt, for example, are men of phase twenty-three —

This man wipes his breath from the window-pane and laughs in his delight at all the varied scene.[70]

But the antithetical (subjective) man, men like Yeats himself, must deliberately adopt the Mask, an image of all that is opposite to his daily life, and of all that he wishes to become. This conception of Anti-Self leads Yeats, a man by nature gregarious, argumentative, and given to political propaganda, to a lonely, austere, impersonal art, celebrating in his poetry the fisherman, the tower, or the wild swans at Coole. In his own phase, seventeen, he also places Dante, Landor and Shelley; the first two have already been mentioned in relation to *Ego Dominus Tuus*, as men who attained to Unity of Being by subjecting will to an impersonal mask; their art becomes "a vision of reality." Shelley, with his passion for reforming the world, never resolved the conflict between his own subjective personality and external reality. In Yeats's terms, he lacked the visions of Evil; his political enemies (unlike Byron's) are monstrous, meaningless images. Thus much of his poetry, fine poet though he was, degenerates into rhetoric — "for what is rhetoric but the will trying to do the work of the imagination?" To prove that Yeats has escaped from Romantic frustration, one need only compare his lyric "*I saw a staring virgin stand*" with the same theme as handled by Shelley in the concluding chorus of *Hellas*.[71]

The most valuable aspect of *A Vision* is not, however, the doctrine of the mask, but rather the coherent symbolic background it provides Yeats's poetic imagination. He has constructed a system of references which impart at once a richness of allusion and a compactness of phrasing to his later work. Whatever one may think of *A Vision* as a philosophical treatise, as a treasure-house for symbols it is invaluable.

Two Songs from a Play illustrate the distilled intensity of Yeats's style at its very best.

Two Songs from a Play

I

I saw a staring virgin stand
Where holy Dionysus died,
And tear the heart out of his side,
And lay the heart upon her hand
And bear that beating heart away;
And then did all the Muses sing
Of Magnus Annus in the spring,
As though God's death were but a play.

Another Troy must rise and set,
Another lineage feed the crow,
Another Argo's painted prow
Drive to a flashier bauble yet.
The Roman Empire stood appalled:
It dropped the reins of peace and war
When that fierce virgin and her Star
Out of the fabulous darkness called.

II

In pity for man's darkening thought
He walked that room and issued thence
In Galilean turbulence;
The Babylonian starlight brought

PUBLICATION OF "A VISION"

> A fabulous, formless darkness in;
> Odor of blood when Christ was slain
> Made all Platonic tolerance vain
> And vain all Doric discipline.
>
> Everything that man esteems
> Endures a moment or a day.
> Love's pleasure drives his love away,
> The painter's brush consumes his dreams;
> The herald's cry, the soldier's tread
> Exhaust his glory and his might:
> Whatever flames upon the night
> Man's own resinous heart has fed.

The symbolism is sufficiently obvious to guarantee a response in the average intelligent reader. At the same time, there is an added subtlety and a depth, of meaning in these two poems which require close analysis. Yeats here demands of his readers not a knowledge of *A Vision*, but certainly a close acquaintance with his thought-symbolism as expressed in other poems. By reference to *A Vision*, one can work backwards and find how closely Yeats follows his own thought — that is, what confidence he has in his own symbols. The moment described in the first poem is the transition from classical civilization to the Christian Era — the influx of the irrational Dionysiac force upon the ordered world of the preceding 2000-year cycle. At the same time the Galilean turbulence, with its odor of blood, is but a reassertion of that primary force which had lain dormant in the Apollonian culture of the West. Christianity is envisaged as a reaction, the fabulous, formless darkness looming up out of the East, from a Babylonian starlight (see *Understanding Poetry*, by Brooks and Warren, p. 614, for a more complete analysis of these two songs).

In *Leda and the Swan* we find Yeats going back two thousand years to the miracle which ushered in classical civilization — the Dove of the Annunciation becomes the Swan —

> A Shudder in the loins engenders there
> The broken wall, the burning roof and tower
> And Agamemnon dead.

The children begotten on Leda, one remembers, were Helen and the Gemini, Castor and Pollux. From one of her eggs came Love and from the other War. Classical civilization runs its allotted course — a predominantly Western, antithetical culture. Then out of the East comes an influx of the primary, then the irrational cry — "the Babe, the Babe is Born." The crucifixion of Christ

PUBLICATION OF "A VISION"

> Made all Platonic tolerance vain
> And vain all Doric discipline.

Each age unwinds the thread the other age has wound. Now in our own time Christianity approaches the completion of its 2000-year span and one remembers Yeats's earlier poem, *The Second Coming* —

> What rough beast, its hour come round at last
> Slouches toward Bethlehem to be born?

This view of civilization is not unique. One finds a similar conception in Nietzsche's distinction between the Apollonian and the Dionysian, and a striking parallel in Spengler's metaphor of the seasons in the *Decline of the West*. But Yeats's thought is his own, and the intensity it lends to his poetry is its own justification. If at times it leads to eloquent despair —

> Man is in love and loves what vanishes
> What more is there to say? [72]

The despair is justified in the civilized European of today. Aware of his isolation in the chaos of the modern world, Yeats has buttressed his thought with a vision. He does not turn his back on his own times, but he holds up against it a picture of a past grandeur. Aware that all is flux, as an artist he tries to fix his eyes on what is permanent in a world governed by change. And he has found that the only permanence is in the change. —

> All things fall and are built again
> And those that build them again are gay.[73]

There is an almost tragic joy in Yeats's conception of a civilization as a struggle to keep self-control. Toward the close of a historical epoch comes "first a sinking in upon the moral being, then the last surrender, the irrational cry, revelation — the scream of Juno's peacock.[74] Out of this comes one consolation:

> It amuses one to remember that before Phidias, and his westward-moving art, Persia fell, and that when the full moon came round again, amid eastward-moving thought, and brought Byzantine glory, Rome fell; and that at the outset of our westward-moving Renaissance Byzantium fell; all things dying each other's life, living each other's death.[75]

It follows from Yeats's system that the climax of a civilization comes at the full moon — its fifteenth phase. It is this imaginative reshaping of the past which gives

PUBLICATION OF "A VISION"

Yeats his most powerful symbol, a symbol which becomes to him that of the heavenly city of the mind —

And therefore I have sailed the seas and come
To the Holy City of Byzantium.

In *A Vision* we find a passage which throws light on the powerful hold this symbol exercises over Yeats's imagination.

"I think if I could be given a month of Antiquity and leave to spend it where I chose, I would spend it in Byzantium a little before Justinian opened St. Sophia and closed the Academy of Plato. I think I could find in some little wine-shop some philosophical worker in mosaic who could answer all my questions, the supernatural descending nearer to him than to Plotinus even, for the pride of his delicate skill would make what was an instrument of power to princes and clerics, a murderous madness in the mob, show as a lovely flexible presence like that of a perfect human body.

I think that in early Byzantium, maybe never before or since in recorded history, religious, aesthetic and practical life were one, that architect and artificers . . . spoke to the multitude and to the few alike. The painter, the mosaic worker, the worker in gold and silver, the illuminator of sacred books, were almost impersonal, almost without the consciousness of individual design, absorbed in their subject matter and that vision of the whole people." [76]

SAILING TO BYZANTIUM

This is the old dream of Unity of Culture, which Yeats in his youth planned to bring to pass in Ireland. The irony and the power of such a poem as *Sailing to Byzantium* arises from our knowledge that the poet is *not* in Byzantium but in Ireland — as Cleanth Brooks has remarked in his essay on *A Vision* (Southern Review, Summer, 1938).

Sailing to Byzantium

I

That is no country for old men. The young
In one another's arms, birds in the trees,
— Those dying generations — at their song,
The salmon-falls, the mackerel-crowded seas,
Fish, flesh, or foul, commend all summer long
Whatever is begotten, born, or dies.
Caught in that sensual music all neglect
Monuments of unageing intellect.

II

An aged man is but a paltry thing,
A tattered coat upon a stick, unless
Soul clap its hands and sing, and louder sing
For every tatter in its mortal dress,
Nor is there any singing school but studying
Monuments of its own magnificence;
And therefore I have sailed the seas and come
To the holy city of Byzantium.

PUBLICATION OF "A VISION"

III

O sages standing in God's holy fire
As in the gold mosaic of a wall,
Come from the holy fire, pern in a gyre,
And be the singing masters of my soul.
Consume my heart away; sick with desire
And fastened to a dying animal
It knows not what it is; and gather me
Into the artifice of eternity.

IV

Once out of nature I shall never take
My bodily form from any natural thing,
But such a form as Grecian goldsmiths make
Of hammered gold and gold enamelling
To keep a drowsy Emperor awake;
Or set upon a golden bough to sing
To lords and ladies of Byzantium
Of what is past, or passing, or to come.

In one of his early essays Yeats laments that "the old resting-places of the mind have been swept away." [77] Now in his old age he reconstructs in his mind's eye an imaginative reality of Being and opposes it to the World of Becoming. The first stanza of this poem poses this conflict in concrete images of creation and decay — lovers in one another's arms, birds mating, the spawning salmon, mackerel-crowded seas; sensual music predominates over the really Real — monuments of unageing intellect. The second stanza brings us to the dominant theme, Yeats's noble protest against the inroads of old age. He attempts to substitute, by an imaginative tour de force, an intellectual art, "gathered into the artifice of eternity," for the complexity and mire of human veins. The sages standing in God's holy fire are the souls of the dead, and fire in Neo-Platonic doctrine is the fifth, heavenly element which purges the grossness of the other four natural, terrestrial elements. Out of this fire was said to be born a bird, and this bird is apparently the bird of the last stanza, "not a natural thing," that is set upon the golden bough.[78] As I understand this poem, it is a fusion of the philosophy of the *Phaedo*, where Socrates maintains that all life is a preparation for death, and two remarks of Blake which linger in Yeats's mind — "The artists are in eternity," and "All antinomies are solved at the bottom of the grave."[79]

To many critics, Yeats's two Byzantium poems are the high-water mark of his intellectual and poetic progress, the perfection of his art. Fine as these poems are, however, I feel that Yeats has pushed his thought into a very rarified atmosphere, and that he creates a white-heat intensity impossible to sustain. Yeats himself was at all times too alive to the world about him to abandon it completely in favor of the artifice of eternity. The poems which follow *Byzantium* are not an anti-climax, but form a healthy complement to that side of Yeats's personality which the Byzantium poems embody. Yeats possessed the happy faculty of never becoming the slave of his style or of his thought. In *A Vision* he felt the lure of metaphysics, but he remained to the last a poet. Who does not mistrust complete ideas? In *Among School Children*, a poem written between the two Byzantium pieces, Yeats embodies an emotion almost the direct antithesis of that expressed in those poems. Escorted through a convent-school by a kind old nun, his mind wanders to a tale told him above a sinking fire by Maud Gonne, "of a harsh reproof or trivial event . . . that changed some childish day to tragedy." Gazing out over the schoolchildren, he wonders if Maud Gonne once looked like one of these:

> And thereupon my heart is driven wild
> She stands before me as a living child.

SAILING TO BYZANTIUM

He ponders his old age, and sees himself as a comfortable kind of old scarecrow. Birth, Life, and Death, all those mysteries solved so neatly in *A Vision*, come again to trouble Yeats's mind. He dismisses good-naturedly the thought of Plato and Aristotle — *Habe nun ach! Philosophie* — did not they too become old scarecrows? — and turns to contemplate the living scene before him. Can one separate the images those nuns worship from the Divinity the images symbolize? Are not all abstractions, the Real and the Ideal, self-born mockers of man's enterprise?

> Grau, teurer Freund, ist alle Theorie,
> Und grün des Lebens goldner Baum.

In the final stanza, the poet takes his stand amid the rich confusion of life. In this, perhaps his finest poem, Yeats states his creed as an artist:

Labour is blossoming or dancing where
The body is not bruised to pleasure soul,
Nor beauty born out of its own despair,
Nor blear-eyed wisdom out of midnight oil.
O chestnut tree, great rooted blossomer,
Are you the leaf, the blossom, or the bole?
O body swayed to music, O brightening glance,
How can we know the dancer from the dance?

V

I AM OF IRELAND

Much of the foregoing analysis of Yeats's development was written before his recent death in France, and while the poet was still alive and writing. His latest poetry can now be viewed in relation to his whole life, and more general conclusions must be drawn. When one contemplates Yeats's career in Ireland and its broader significance, a passage he wrote long ago comes to mind:

> I have been busy with a single art, that of . . . a small, unpopular theater; and this art may well seem to practical men, busy with some program of industrial or political regeneration, of no more account than the shaping of an agate; and yet in the shaping of an agate, whether in the cutting or in the making of the design, one discovers, if one have a speculative mind, thoughts that seem important and principles that may be applied to life itself, and certainly if one does not believe so, one is but a poor cutter of so hard a stone.[80]

All of Yeats's lifelong preoccupation with style, symbolism, and "the arts," was it, after all, but the cutting of an agate? I think not. Yeats's career in public life dismisses at once the accusation that he retired into the seclusion of an Ivory Tower. On the other hand, one can hardly agree with such critics as Mr. Leavis, who claims that "Yeats's poetry was but a marginal commentary on his life." [81] The apparent contradictions in Yeats's career can be resolved if one but remembers that he was at once an Irishman, vitally concerned in "the seeming needs of my fool-driven land," and a man who never forgot that it was his first business in life to be a poet. From his early youth he realized that "We make out of the quarrel with others rhetoric, out of the quarrel with ourselves poetry." [82]

And so, in his lonely Norman Tower at Thoor Ballylee, itself a symbol of that side of his personality which he holds aloof from the hurly-burly of everyday life, Yeats writes poems permeated with the amazing vigor of his old age. He once announced that he would dine at journey's end with Landor and with Donne. Now, however, it becomes apparent that his thought has turned in another direction:

I AM OF IRELAND

I declare this tower is my symbol; I declare
This winding, gyring, spiring treadmill of a
  stair is my ancestral chair;
That Goldsmith and the Dean, Berkeley and
  Burke have traveled there.

It is plain that Yeats — always a proud man — has reserved a place for himself among "the indomitable Irishry." . . .

Berkeley with his belief in perception, that abstract ideas are mere words, Swift with his love of perfect nature, of the Houyhnhnms, his disbelief in Newton's system and every sort of machine, Goldsmith and his delight in the particulars of common life that shocked his contemporaries, Burke with his conviction that all states not grown slowly like a forest tree are tyrannies, found in England the opposite that made their thought lucid and stung it into expression.[83]

Add to this group Parnell — the tragic figure of a proud, lonely individual crushed by participation in politics — and these are the men about whom Yeats has focused his imagination. One notes that the particular traits Yeats singles out in these men are perhaps more characteristic of Yeats himself. But all, including Yeats, have one thing in common — are they not of that remarkable, isolated breed, *Hiberniores Hibernicis ipsis?* Who is the true Irishman?

SAILING TO BYZANTIUM

Had Yeats's poetic production ceased with *The Tower* (1928), his stylistic development could be plotted along a relatively straight, ascending line. His art proceeds from the loose, shimmering, Romantic verse of *Innisfree* and *Who Will Go Drive With Fergus Now?* to the severe, Classical intensity of *Byzantium* and *Nineteen Hundred and Nineteen*. Yeats once told Ezra Pound that he had spent his whole life stripping his poetry of "the poetic," of what Wordsworth before him had called "gaudy and inane phraseology." [84] And Yeats succeeded better than Wordsworth in getting back to "the language really used by men," to living speech rhythms:

> Repentance keeps my heart impure;
> But what am I that dare
> Fancy that I can
> Better conduct myself or have more
> Sense than a common man? [85]

At the same time, however, the exfoliation of Yeats's style was accompanied by the evolution of a symbolic pattern which gives his later poetry its unique intensity, its tone of authority. There is a certain aloofness, almost bitterness, that permeates much of his best poetry. As Stephen Spender complains, although Yeats feels his thought as immediately as a rose, too often his thoughts are "very aristocratic cabbage roses" [86] — courtesy, the ceremony of innocence, aristocratic breeding, and a scorn of the common lot of mankind. Part of Yeats's hostility to democratic bonhomie is the result of his bitter experiences in Dublin, which lead him to read Castiglione and long for "the green shadow of Ferrara wall." The rest must be attributed to his own temperament; Yeats has always loved the word "arrogant."

But the poetry of the last decade of Yeats's life restores a healthy balance to his collected work; it reveals a more complete approach to humanity. After the "breathless starlit air" of *Byzantium*, one can the better enjoy such lines as:

> What shall I do for pretty girls,
> Now my old bawd is dead? [87]

Yeats substitutes the antics of Crazy Jane for the golden smithies of the emperor, and the change is all to the good. Bawdy is the only word which adequately describes the humorous garrulity of many poems in *Words For Music Perhaps* and the latest poetry.

Yeats has come down from his "high stilts" to proclaim "What theme had Homer but Original Sin?"[88] In 1909 Yeats wrote in his diary:

> All my life I have been haunted by the idea that the poet should know all classes of men. . . . He will play with all Masks.[89]

This accounts for the right about-face in the latest work. Yeats knew all classes of men, but he never truckled to what another distinguished Dubliner termed middle-class morality. Hence when Yeats drops the aristocratic tone, he descends to what the middle-class calls "the vulgar":

> And he went in and she went on
> And both climbed up the stair
> And O he was a clever man
> For he his slippers wore,
> And when they came to the top stair
> He ran on ahead
> His wife he found and the rich man
> In the comfort of a bed.
> *The Colonel went out sailing.*[90]

This lighter poetry serves as a catharsis, a welcome intrusion of the humorous and the profane into the fastidious atmosphere of the work which preceded it. Yeats has not abandoned his symbols, but he can take them less seriously:

I AM OF IRELAND

> What made the ceiling waterproof?
> Landor's tarpaulin on the roof.[91]

Or we hear him pronounce them "all metaphor, Malachi, stilts and all." [92] Now and then, however, Yeats can summon up his symbols with all their old intensity, as in *Parnell's Funeral*.[93] Even in this poem it is significant that the symbols have been transplanted from Byzantium to Ireland. In the finest of his later lyrics, *I Am of Ireland*, Yeats has evolved a more general and universal symbolism. This poem may be taken as a final commentary. A perfect expression of the wisdom and sympathy which shines out in the poet's old age, it catches at the same time a definitely tragic emotion:

> 'I am of Ireland,
> And the Holy Land of Ireland,
> And time runs on,' cried she.
> 'Come out of charity
> And dance with me in Ireland.'
>
> * * *
>
> 'The fiddlers are all thumbs
> Or the fiddle-string accursed,
> The drums and the kettledrums
> And the trumpets are all burst,
> And the trombone,' cried he,
> 'The trumpet and the trombone,'
> And cocked a malicious eye,
> 'But time runs on, runs on.'

SAILING TO BYZANTIUM

> 'I am of Ireland,
> And the Holy Land of Ireland,
> And time runs on,' cried she.
> 'Come out of charity
> And dance with me in Ireland.'

Keats has said that a man's life of any worth is a continual allegory. In this age of reasons and purposes, one is often asked "Why read Yeats?" For philosophy one can indeed go elsewhere. Yeats never succeeded in rationalizing his own impulses and intuitions, not even in *A Vision*. His greatness consists solely in this — out of the quarrel with himself he made poetry. It is as a poet, a master craftsman, that Yeats's name is honored today. The poets sing amidst their uncertainty, and the younger poets of today, going their separate ways, can sing more confidently with Yeats's achievement stirring them to emulation. No finer tribute has been paid to Yeats's memory than the memorial elegy of W. H. Auden, who "pardons him for writing well." In the influence of the older poet upon the younger, one can see today a hope for poetry:

> He disappeared in the dead of winter.
> The brooks were frozen, the airports almost deserted,

I AM OF IRELAND

And snow disfigured the public statues;
The mercury sank in the mouth of the dying day.
O all the instruments agree
The day of his death was a dark cold day. . . .

Now he is scattered among a hundred cities,
And wholly given over to unfamiliar affections;
To find his happiness in another kind of wood,
And be punished under a foreign code of conscience:
The words of a dead man
Are modified in the guts of the living.

But in the importance and noise of Tomorrow
When the brokers are roaring like beasts on the floor of the Burse,
And the poor have their sufferings to which they are fairly accustomed,
And each in the cell of himself is almost convinced of his freedom,
A few thousand will think of this day,
As one thinks of a day when one did something slightly unusual.
He was silly like us: His gift survived it all.

O all the instruments agree
The day of his death was a dark cold day.

NOTES

NOTES

Quotations from the works of William Butler Yeats are made by special permission of the Macmillan Company, holders of the copyright.

1. James Joyce: *A Portrait of the Artist as a Young Man.* Modern Library Ed., p. 297.
2. W. B. Yeats: *Essays.* Preface, p. 1.
3. Forrest Reid: *W. B. Yeats: A Critical Study*, p. 18.
4. *Autobiographies:* p. 135.
5. George Moore: *Vale*, p. 211.
6. *Autobiographies:* p. 131.
7. Asst. Prof. W. E. Houghton (lecture).
8. R. L. Stevenson: *Collected Letters*, vol. IV, p. 299. Edited by Sidney Colvin. Skerrymore Edition.
9. Stephen Spender: *The Destructive Element*, p. 47. Also *Spectator*, 2/23/34.
10. P. E. More: *Shelburne Essays*, vol. I, p. 177.
11. *Ibid.*, p. 179.
12. George Moore: *Vale*, pp. 160–174.
13. *Essays:* p. 6.
14. George Moore: *Vale*, p. 172.
15. *A Vision*, p. 157.
16. *Autobiographies*, p. 101.
17. *Ibid.*, p. 146.
18. J. M. Synge: *Preface* to *The Playboy of the Western World*, p. 1.
19. *Collected Poems:* p. 103.
20. *Ibid.*, p. 106.

NOTES

21. There is a possible fourth factor in that Ezra Pound and the Imagists began publishing their critical manifestoes in 1912. Yeats in his *Essays* (p. 178) tells us:

> Some seven or eight years ago I asked my friend Ezra Pound to point out everything in the language of my poems he thought in abstraction, and I learned from him how much farther the movement against abstraction had gone than my generation had thought possible. (1924)

I do not think, however, that Pound exerted any influence on Yeats before 1915, and little thereafter. The whole movement of modern poetry away from the Nineteenth Century was then in full swing.

22. T. S. Eliot: *The Use of Poetry.*

23. John Keats: Letter to George Keats, Mar. 13, 1819.

24. T. S. Eliot: *After Strange Gods*, p. 41.

25. *Autobiographies:* p. 303; also p. 301.

26. W. B. Yeats: *The Countess Cathleen.*

27. W. B. Yeats: Introduction to *Selections from Irish Authors* (1895).

28. These random remarks are recorded in *The Portrait of the Artist as a Young Man*, p. 266. Joyce was apparently present at the performance.

29. Yeats was not present at the opening performance. He appeared, however, on the second night.

30. *Essays:* p. 372.

31. *Ibid.*, p. 354.

32. *Autobiographies:* p. 178.

33. *Coll. Poems:* p. 71.

NOTES

34. *Autobiographies:* p. 91.
35. *A Vision:* p. 132.
36. *Coll. Poems:* p. 118.
37. Maud Gonne Macbride: *A Servant of the Queen*, p. 329.
38. *Essays*, p. 188.
39. Yeats never speaks of having met Mallarmé. Arthur Symons read the French poets to Yeats in translation.
40. P. E. More: *Shelburne Essays*, vol. I, p. 178.
41. Mallarmé: Quoted by Louis MacNeice: *Modern Poetry*, p. 101.
42. W. B. Yeats: *Wheels and Butterflies*, p. 91.
43. Cf. *Axel's Castle*, pp. 26 seq.
44. K. Quinn: *Blake and the New Age*. Virginia Quarterly Review, 4/27, p. 310.
45. Cf. E. M. Tillyard: *Poetry: Direct and Oblique*, p. 38. (A confusion of the emotional with the intellectual symbol.)

> The basic idea of symbolism is that ideally all words should be given the charge of meaning born by Blake's *rose* or Keats's *alien* in " alien corn."

46. The phrase is Edmund Wilson's, *Axel's Castle*, p. 28.
47. *Essays:* p. 191.
48. *Autobiographies:* p. 284.
49. C. Day Lewis: *A Hope For Poetry*, p. 65.
50. I. A. Richards: *Principles of Literary Criticism*, p. 197; *Science and Poetry*, p. 85.
51. *Coll. Poems:* p. 292.
52. Cf. Mary Colum: *Saturday Review of Lit.*, 2/25/39, p. 3.

NOTES

53. Ezra Pound quotes a remark of Charles Ricketts' which pleased Yeats:

Oh Yeats, what a pity they can't all be beaten! *Kulcher*, p. 188.

54. Cf. AE, contemporary reviews collected in *The Living Torch* (1914–1925).

55. This view is similar to that expressed by T. S. Eliot in *The Sacred Wood:* p. 58.

Poetry is not a turning loose of emotion, but an escape from emotion; it is not the expression of personality, but an escape from personality.

56. *Autobiographies:* p. 235.

57. The doctrine is similar to that expounded by Keats in his passage on Negative Capability. *Letters:* to George Keats, 12/28/1817, to R. Woodhouse, 10/27/1818.

58. *Coll. Poems:* p. 215.

59. *Ibid.:* p. 452, note.

60. *Ibid.:* p. 238.

61. *Ibid.:* p. 452, note.

62. An explanation of the symbolism of this poem was later published in *A Vision*, pp. 207–8.

63. *Last Will and Testament* of Auden and Macneice, from *Letters from Iceland*.

64. H. Reynolds: *Letters to the New Island*, Intro., p. 20.

65. W. B. Yeats: Introduction to *Berkeley*, by Hone and Rossi. London, 1931.

66. *A Packet for Ezra Pound:* pp. 8–10.

67. *Ibid.:* p. 8.

68. *A Vision:* p. 35.

69. *Ibid.:* p. 80.

70. *Ibid.:* p. 165.

NOTES

71. Cf. E. Tillyard's comparison of these two pieces in *Poetry: Direct and Oblique*, p. 38, and a rebuttal by D. Bush: *Mythology and the Romantic Tradition*, pp. 163-66.

72. *Coll. Poems:* p. 240.

73. *New Poems* (1938): p. 4.

74. *A Vision:* p. 268.

75. *Ibid.:* p. 270-80.

76. *Ibid.:* p. 279.

77. W. B. Yeats: *Letters to the New Island,* p. 143.

78. Yeats appends the following note to this poem:

> I have read somewhere that in the emperor's palace at Byzantium was a tree made of gold and silver, and artificial birds that sang. (*Coll. Poems*, p. 450.)

For the bird born out of the fire, cf. Yeats's *Essays: Anima Mundi*, p. 512.

79. *Essay on William Blake* (p. 136); also *Wheels and Butterflies:* p. 97.

80. *Preface* to *The Cutting of an Agate:* p. 271.

81. F. R. Leavis: *New Bearings in Modern Poetry*, p. 47.

82. *Essays:* p. 492.

83. Hone and Rossi: *Berkeley*. Intro. by Yeats, p. iv.

84. Cf. also Ezra Pound: *Pavannes and Divisions*, p. 107.

> Mr. Yeats has once and for all stripped English poetry of its perdamnable rhetoric. He has boiled away all that is not poetic, and a great deal that is. . . . He has made our poetic idiom a thing pliable, a speech without inversions.

NOTES

85. *Coll. Poems:* p. 293.
86. Stephen Spender: *The Destructive Element,* p. 39.
87. *The New Republic,* 2/15/39, p. 37.
88. *Coll. Works:* p. 290.
89. *Autobiographies:* p. 401.
90. *New Poems* (1938): p. 16.
91. *The New Republic:* 2/15/39, p. 37.
92. *High Talk. The Nation:* 1/11/39, p. 623.
93. *The King of the Great Clock Tower:* p. 23.

BIBLIOGRAPHY

BIBLIOGRAPHY

A. Original Sources

Yeats, William Butler: *Early Poems and Stories*, New York, 1925.
—— *Plays and Controversies*, New York, 1925.
—— *Plays in Prose and Verse*, New York, 1925.
—— *Letters to the New Island*, Cambridge, Mass., 1934.
—— *Wheels and Butterflies*, New York, 1935.
—— *King of the Great Clock Tower*, New York, 1935.
—— *Preface* to *Oxford Book of Modern Verse*, New York, 1937.
—— *Collected Poems*, New York, 1937.
—— *Autobiographies*, New York, 1938.
—— *A Vision*, New York, 1938.
—— *New Poems*, Cuala Press, Dublin, 1938.

B. Secondary Sources (in Ireland)

Eglinton, John: *Irish Literary Portraits*, Dublin and London, 1935.
Gogarty, O. St. J.: *As I Was Walking Down Sackville Street*, Dublin and London, 1937.
Joyce, James: *A Portrait of the Artist as a Young Man*, London, 1916.
Macbride, Maud G.: *A Servant of the Queen*, London, 1938.
Moore, George: *Hail and Farewell*, London, 1911.
Russell, George: *Letters to Yeats*, Cuala Press, Dublin, 1936.

Russell, George: *Imaginations and Reveries*, Dublin, 1921.
—— *The Living Torch*, London, 1937.

C. Criticism and Biography

Bush, Douglas: *Mythology and the Romantic Tradition*, Cambridge, Mass., 1937.

Eliot, T. S.: *After Strange Gods*, New York, 1934.
—— *The Use of Poetry*, Cambridge, Mass., 1933.

Empson, William: *Seven Types of Ambiguity*, London, 1930.

Hone, J. M.: *William Butler Yeats: Poet in Contemporary Ireland*, Dublin, 1916.

Leavis, F. R.: *New Bearings in Modern Poetry*, London, 1935.

Lewis, C. Day: *A Hope For Poetry*, London, 1937.

Pollock, J. H.: *William Butler Yeats*, London, 1935.

Pound, Ezra: *Pavannes and Divisions*, New York, 1918.

Reid, Forrest: *William Butler Yeats: A Critical Study*, New York, 1915.

Richards, I. A.: *Science and Poetry*, New York, 1926.
—— *Principles of Literary Criticism*, London, 1934.

Spender, Stephen: *The Destructive Element*, London, 1935.

Tate, Allen: *Reactionary Essays on Poetry and Ideas*, New York, 1937.

Tillyard, E. M.: *Poetry: Direct and Oblique*, London, 1934.

Wilson, Edmund: *Axel's Castle*, New York, 1936.

Wrenn, C. L.: *William Butler Yeats: A Literary Study*, Durham Univ. Journal, 1920.

BIBLIOGRAPHY

D. Periodical Reviews (chronological)

Colum, Padraic: *Yale Review*, January, 1925, pp. 381–385.

Wilson, Edmund: *New Republic*, October 5, 1927, pp. 176–177.

Spencer, Theo.: *New Republic*, October 10, 1928, pp. 219–220.

—— *Nation-Athenaeum*, April 21, 1928, p. 80.

O'Faolain, Sean: *New Criterion*, April, 1930, pp. 523–528.

Matthiesson, F. O.: *Yale Review*, Spring, 1934, pp. 611–617.

Blackmur, R. P.: *Amer. Mercury*, February, 1934, p. 244.

—— *Southern Review*, Summer, 1936, pp. 339–362.

Brooks, Cleanth: *Southern Review*, Summer, 1938, pp. 116–142.

Macleish, A.: *Yale Review*, Summer, 1938, pp. 94–110.

Bogan, Louise: *Nation*, February 25, 1939, pp. 234–35.

Auden, W. H.: *New Republic*, March 8, 1939, p. 123.